The Ink-credible Cephalopod Coloring Book

Written and Illustrated by Sarah McAnulty

2018
www.SarahMcAnulty.com

Copyright © Sarah McAnulty 2018
All Rights Reserved

McAnulty, Sarah
The Inkcredible Cephalopod Coloring Book / Sarah McAnulty
ISBN 9781980914464
1. Nature-Animals-Marine Life 2. Science-Life Science-Marine Biology 3. Science-Life Science-Zoology-Invertebrates

Independently published

くコ:彡　　*Dedication*　　くコ:彡

To David F. Jenkins III AKA "Jenkins"

And to Darshu

who always encourage all of my cockamamie plans

Welcome to the World of Cephalopods

Cephalopods (cuttlefish, octopus, squid, and nautilus) are some of the most engaging and visually striking animals on the planet. Their complex behaviors, dazzling color displays, and problem solving abilities have captured the minds of artists and scientists since the earliest human writings, going back to Aristotle. Cephalopods can be found almost anywhere. They thrive in reefs, coastal regions, hydrothermal vents, and even the abyssal plains of the deep ocean. Some people refer to cephalopods as "aliens" but let me get the record straight- these animals are undeniably earthlings. Cephalopods have been on earth for 500 million years-- that's longer than trees or any of the vertebrates! These animals went down a different evolutionary path from humans a LONG time ago, so they're really the most different intelligent life forms from us on this planet. Unlike whales, birds, dogs, and many animals more closely related to us, cephalopods communicate with color instead of sound. They can camouflage in their environment perfectly, mimicking their surroundings with color and shape, despite being colorblind! I could write chapters about the cephalopods, from their mating behavior to their immune cells, but this is a coloring book. There is so much we don't know about cephalopods, but in these pages you'll learn a lot about what we DO know, and get to know many of the world's coolest cephalopod species.

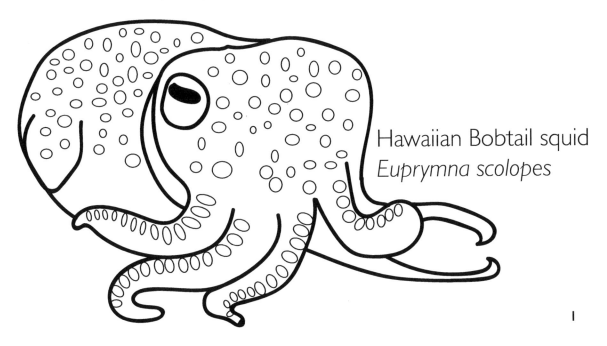

Hawaiian Bobtail squid
Euprymna scolopes

Cephalopod Anatomy

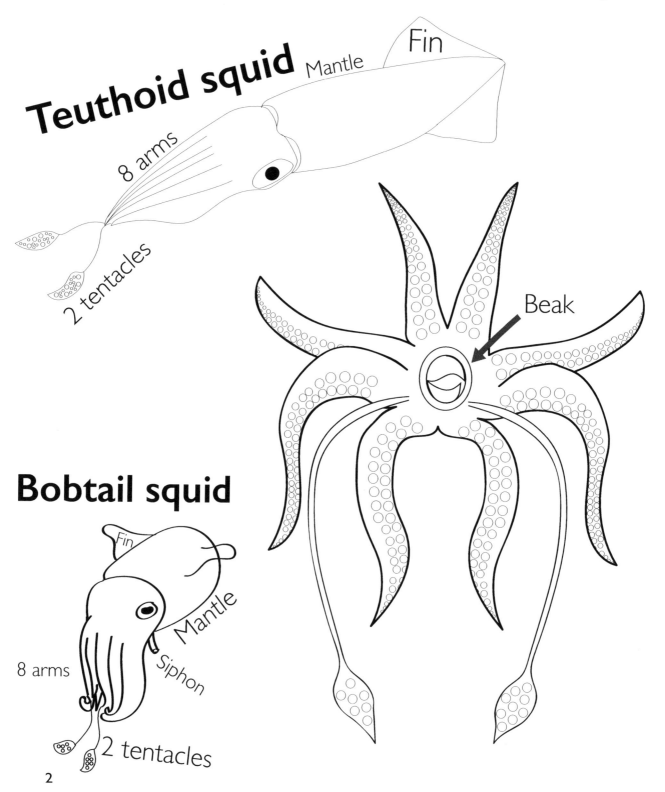

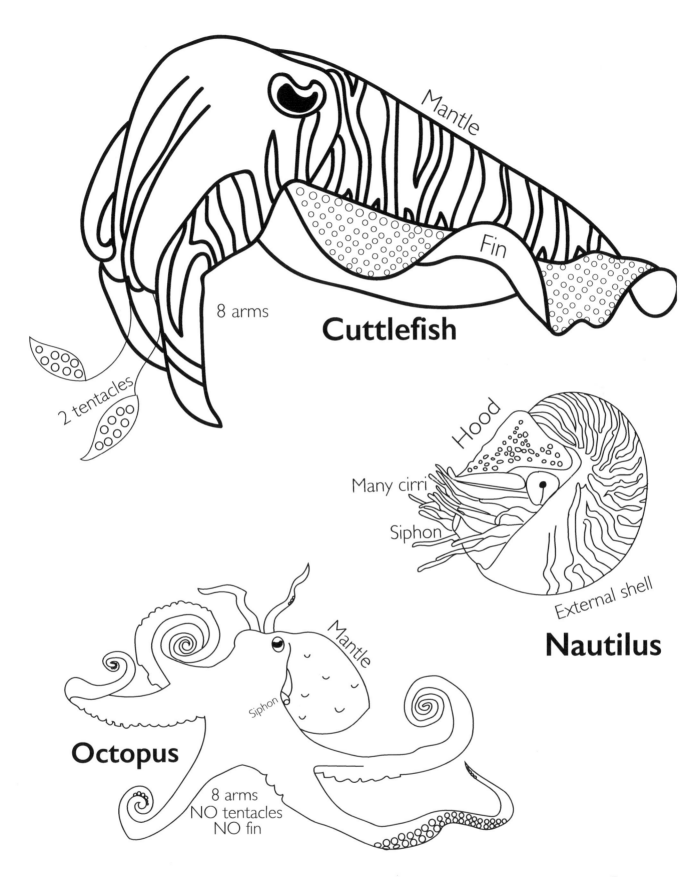

A is for Argonaut

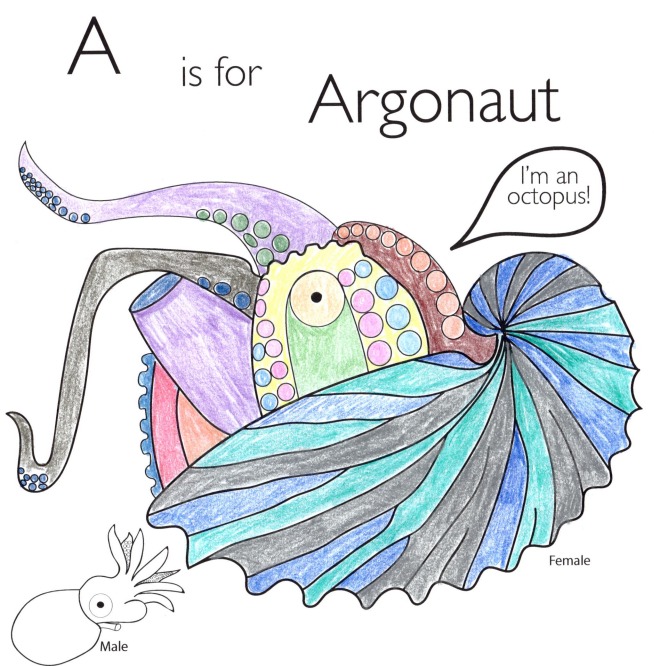

Female argonauts (*Argonauta argo*) make papery shells of calcium carbonate where they keep their eggs. They are sometimes called paper nautiluses (see N is for Nautilus) but they're actually octopuses! Male argonauts are much smaller and don't need to form a shell.

B is for Blanket Octopus

Male

Female

Female blanket octopuses (*Tremoctopus spp.*) are sometimes 10,000 times bigger than male blanket octpuses! When males and females of the same species look different, this is called "**sexual dimorphism**". Blanket octopuses are powerful women in the animal world.

C is for Cuttlefish

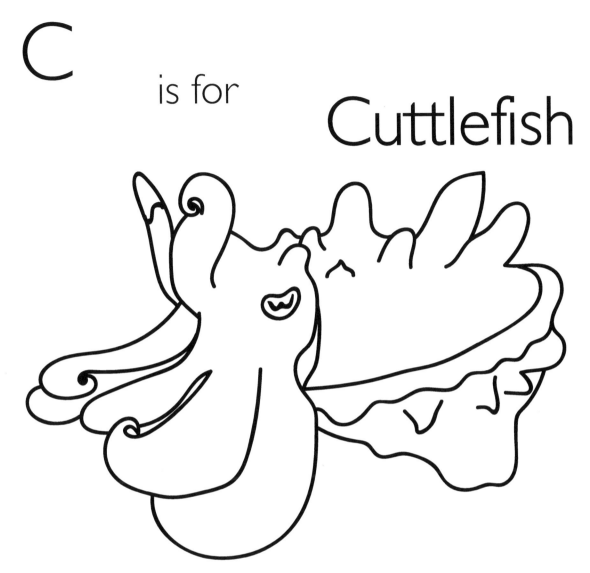

Flamboyant cuttlefish (*Metasepia pfefferi*) can produce complex patterns with color-changing cells in their skin called **chromatophores** (present in most cephalopods). They use bright colors and quickly changing patterns to confuse prey and intimidate predators. Most cuttlefish use their **cuttlebones** to maintain **bouyancy**, preventing them from either floating too much or sinking. The flamboyant cuttlefish's **cuttlebone** is too dense to float, so they mostly walk on the seafloor.

D is for *Dosidicus gigas*

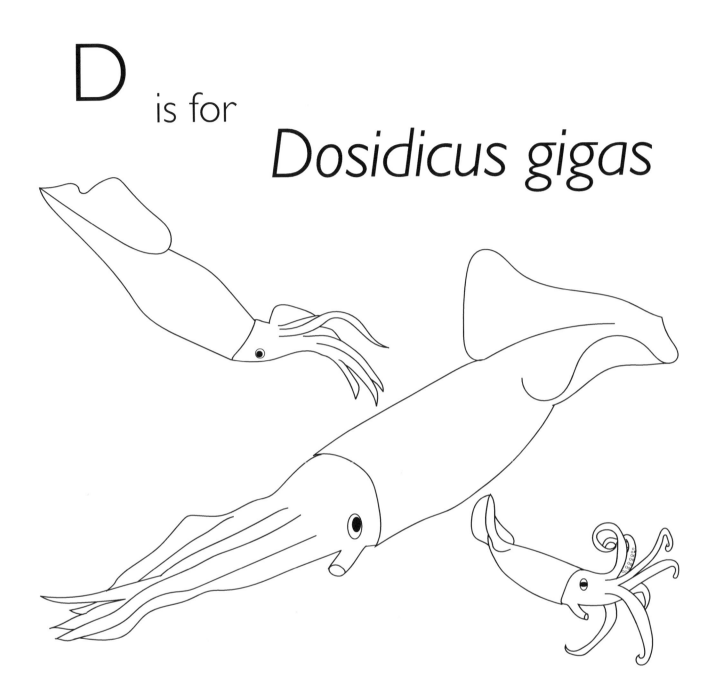

Humboldt squid (*Dosidicus gigas*) are huge — Some grow to 2 meters (6.5 feet). These squid are curious and aggressive and sometimes eat each other. Humboldt squid live in large groups. They flash white and red, possibly to communicate!

E is for *Enteroctopus dofleini*

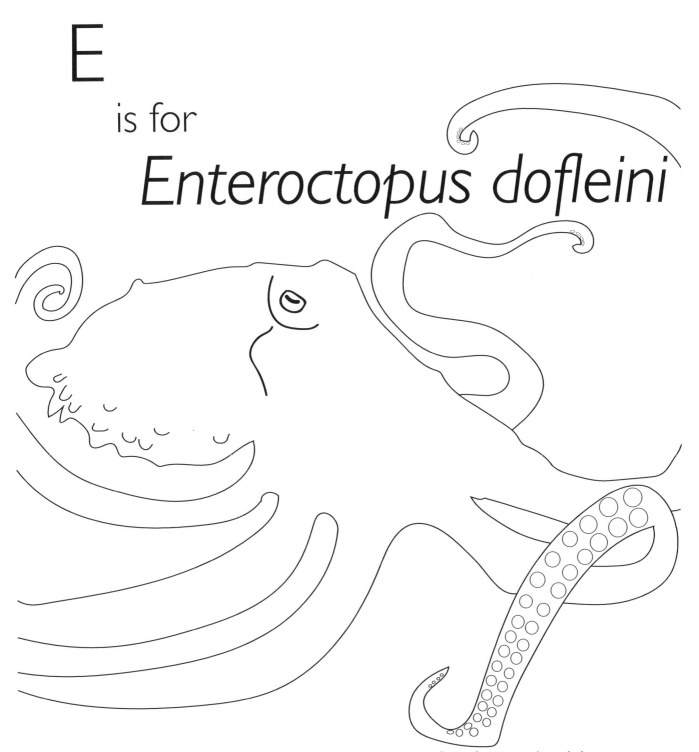

Giant Pacific Octopus (*Enteroctopus dofleini*) are the biggest living octopuses — some are 6 meters (20 feet) across! They're common aquarium octopuses and are notorious escape artists.

F is for Firefly squid

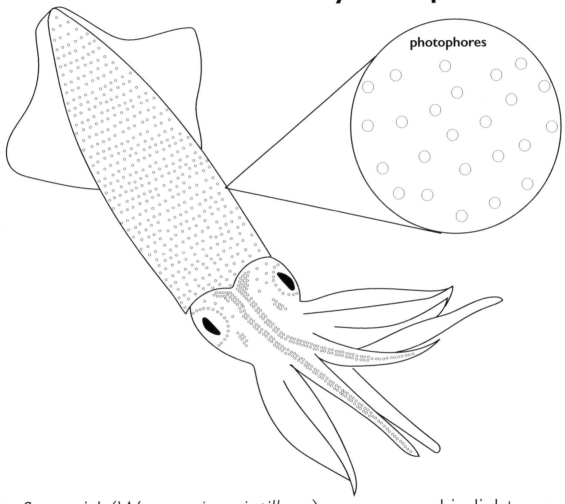

Firefly squid (*Watasenia scintillans*) are covered in light-producing organs called **photophores**. These organs produce **bioluminescence** (light produced by living creatures) in blue and green. Scientists think they do this to find a mate.

Giant squid (*Architeuthis dux*) can reach 13 meters (42 feet) from the tip of their fins to the end of their tentacles. Their mantles can be 2.4 meters (7.8 feet) long. Giant squid were not photographed alive until 2004!

H is for Hawaiian bobtail squid

Hawaiian bobtail squid (*Euprymna scolopes*) are active at night and have a **symbiosis** with glowing **bacteria**! The squid use light from the **bacteria** to make their underside glow match the moonlight from above so predators below can't see them. Scientists use these squid to understand **symbiosis**!

I is for Idiosepius

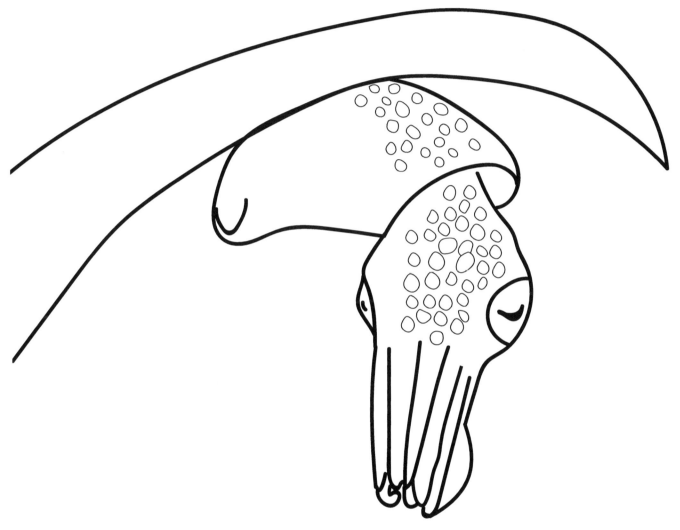

Pygmy squid (*Idiosepius spp.*) are the smallest of all the cephalopods. They have the ability to adhere themselves to underwater plants so that they can hang upside down and blend in to hide from predators!

J is for Japanese Flying Squid

Japanese flying squid (*Todarodes pacificus*) use **jet propsulsion** to shoot out of the water! Air is easier to fly through than water is to swim through, so leaving the water saves energy for the squid when traveling long distances.

K is for Kraken

The fearsome Kraken of old Norse mythology is probably just a giant squid (see G is for Giant squid)! When these animals are dying they sometimes float near the top of the water, (unlike other cephalopods, who sink), which is where sailors likely would have come into contact with these "sea monsters".

L is for Longarm Squid

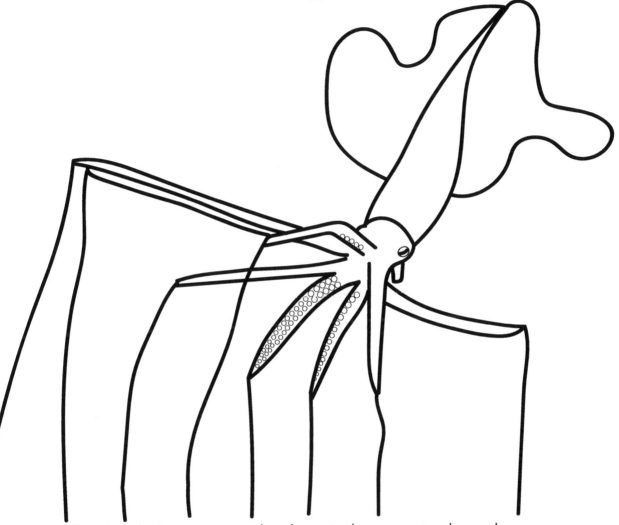

We really don't know much about the mysterious longarm squid, also known as the bigfin squid (*Magnapinna spp.*). What we do know is that they live deep in the ocean — even 3 miles below the surface! Their 8 meter long arms may be used to drag along the seafloor looking for prey.

M is for *Mesonychoteuthis hamiltoni*

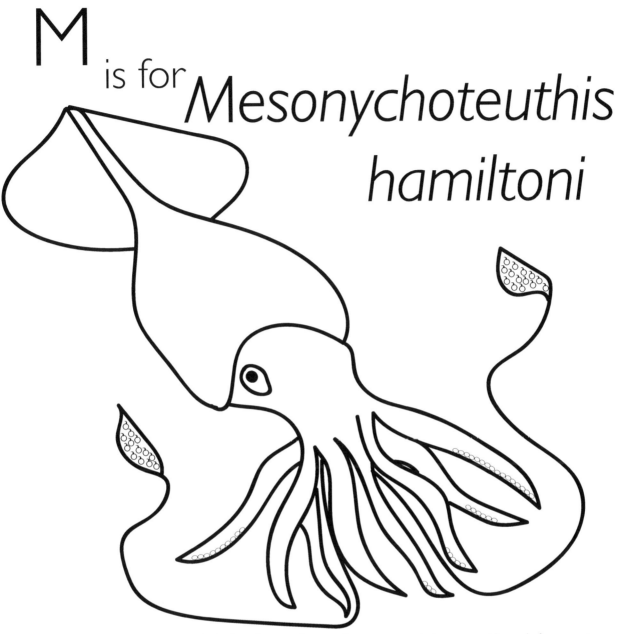

Scientists used to think that the giant squid was the biggest squid on the block, but then the colossal squid (*Mesonychoteuthis hamiltoni*) was discovered. The colossal squid is much thicker bodied than the giant squid and can have 3 meter long mantles. They have been found in the waters around Antarctica. The record-breaking squid was found in 2007.

N is for Nautilus

Nautiluses are friends not decorations!

The nautilus (*Nautilus pompilius*) is one of the most ancient lineages of living cephalopods. Their beautiful zebra-striped shell has led to their decline because people fish them out of the water faster than they can reproduce. Save the nautilus! Never buy nautilus shells!

O is for *Octopus vulgaris*

The common octopus (*Octopus vulgaris*) lives all over the world, from the Mediterranean, to England and Africa. Fisherman consider them rascals becuase they often steal lobsters from traps.

P is for Pyjama squid

The pyjama squid (*Sepioloidea lineolata*) is also called a "dumpling squid" because of its short squat body. These cephalopods live in sand and **seagrass** around Australia and throughout the Indo-Pacific. To hide from predators they often bury themselves in sand. Each squid's stripe pattern is unique, like the squid version of a fingerprint!

Q is for Quick swimmers

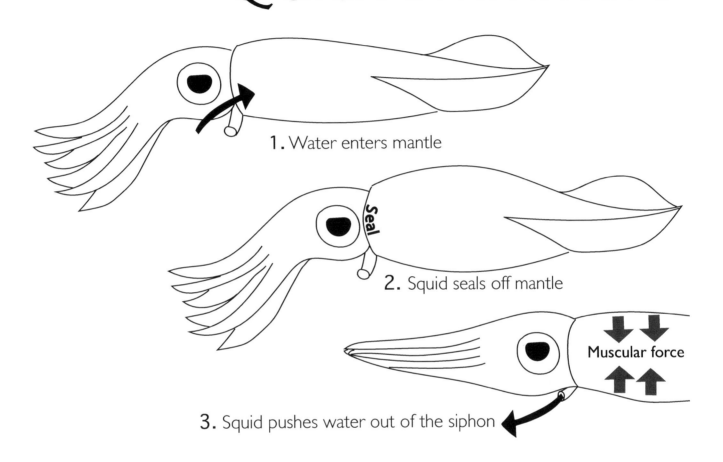

1. Water enters mantle
2. Squid seals off mantle
3. Squid pushes water out of the siphon

Cephalopods swim quickly using **jet propulsion**. They take a deep breath of water into their body, then close off the holes that open to the inside of their body (right behind each eye), then force the seawater out their siphon. This sudden push of water propels their bodies backward and away from danger.

R is for Radula

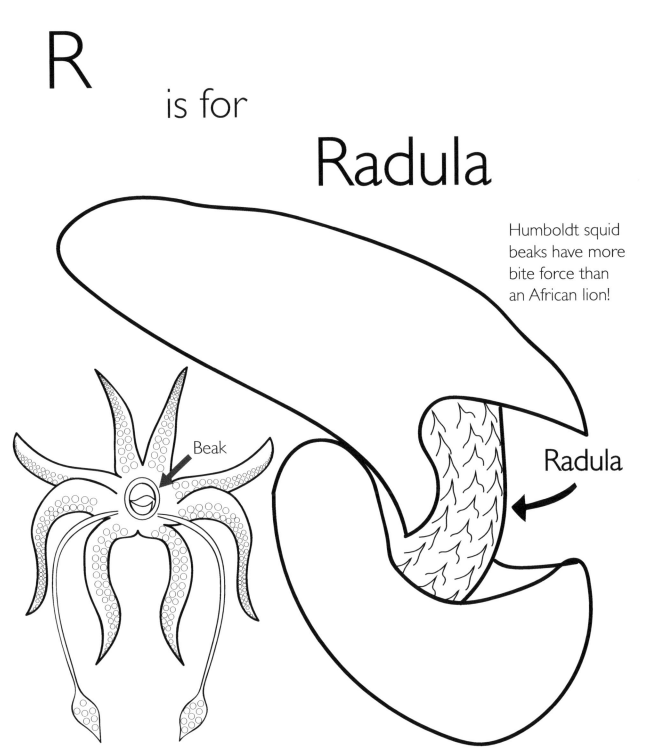

Humboldt squid beaks have more bite force than an African lion!

Instead of a tongue, cephalopods have a **radula** in their **beak**! The radula has small teeth-like structures on its surface which are used to grate the cephalopod's food.

S is for *Sepia apama*

Giant Australian cuttlefish (*Sepia apama*) are the largest of the cuttlefish. These animals can grow to almost a meter in length! In addition to color-changing chromatophores, they can also change their texture using **papillae**. Indeed, big can be beautiful.

T is for Teuthologist

Teuthology is the study of squid! This is Sarah the squid scientist. She works with Hawaiian bobtail squid. She spent so much time thinking about squid she made a coloring book about them.

U is for Uroteuthis

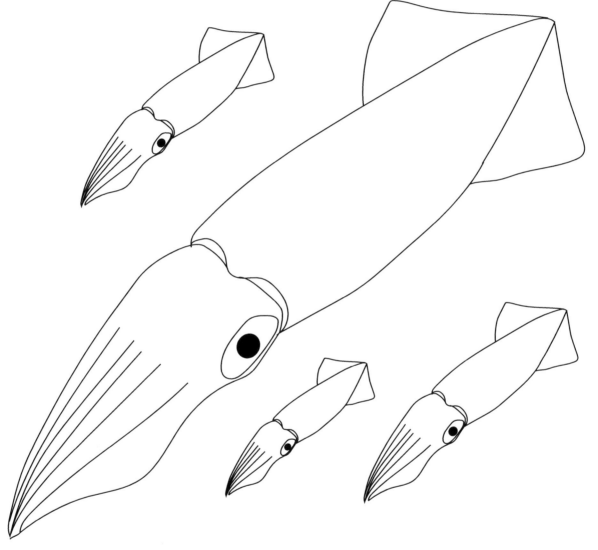

Bartsch's squid (*Uroteuthis bartschi*) live throughout the Indopacific. Much like the Hawaiian bobtail squid they have a light organ where they house bioluminescent bacteria!

V is for Vampire squid

Despite their frightening appearance, the vampire squid (*Vampyroteuthis infernalis*) eats "**marine snow**", which is a collection of dead things and poop that fall from animals living closer to the surface! They also have **bioluminescence** in the tips of their arms and in spots above their eyes so that predators think the vampire squid is larger than they are.

X is for X-rayed squid

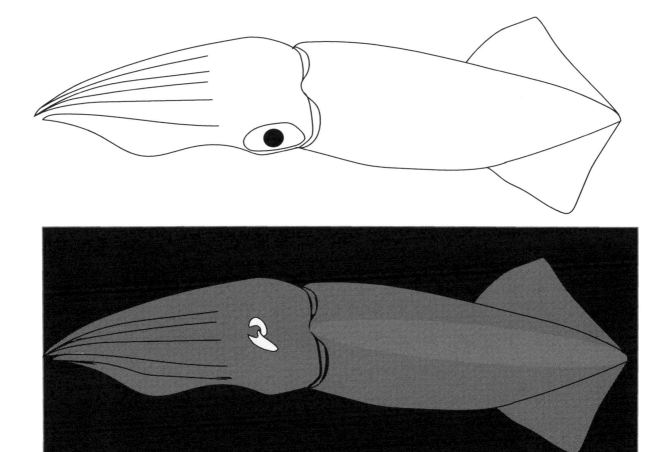

If you looked at a squid in an X-ray you wouldn't see a skeleton because they're invertebrates, or animals without any bones. You'd see a beak, the pen (the squid's internal "shell"), and some other very light structures.

Y is for Youngibelus

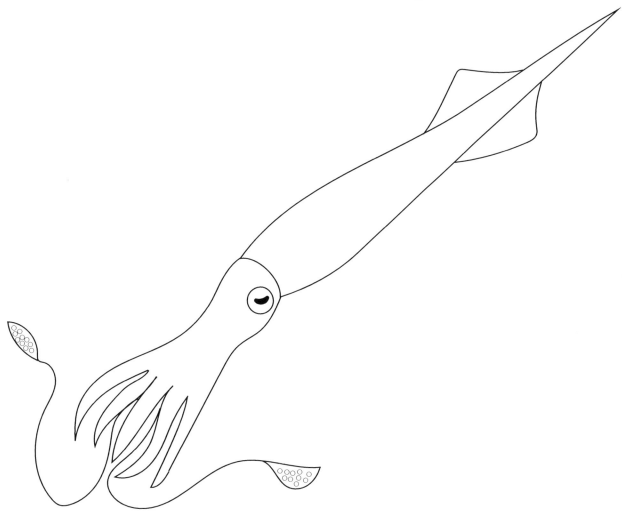

Youngibelus is the only extinct cephalopod in this book! It is a type of **belemnite**, which were the ancestors of the modern day squid and cuttlefish. These squid were alive during the same time period as Stegosaurus and Plesiosaurus!

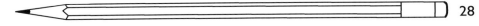

Z is for Zebra-stripes on cuttlefish

When some cuttlefish become adults, they show zebra stripes in displays of **courtship** and aggression. Males have more pronounced stripes than females.

Cephalopod Scale

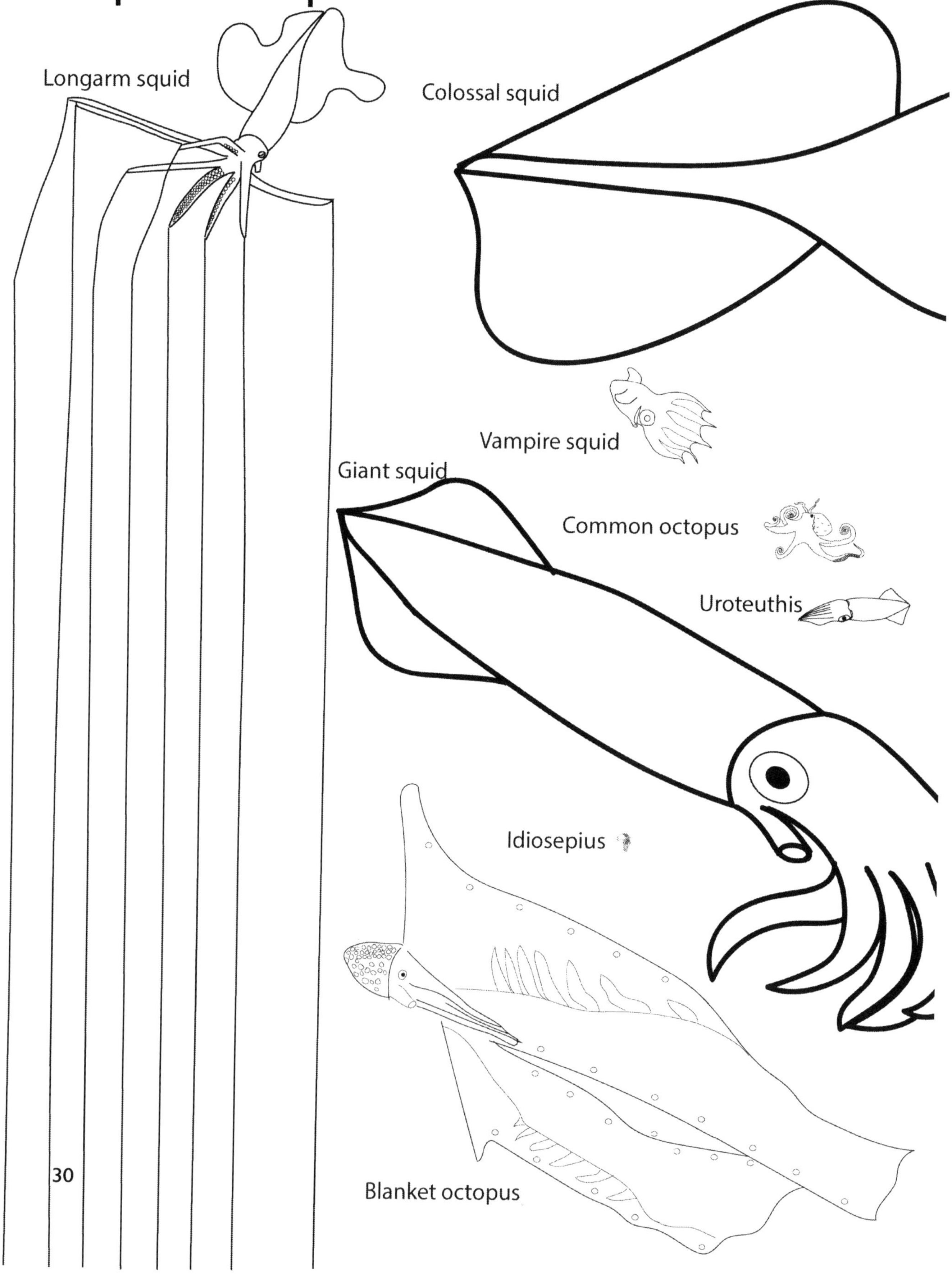

Longarm squid

Colossal squid

Vampire squid

Giant squid

Common octopus

Uroteuthis

Idiosepius

Blanket octopus

Glossary

Arm Octopuses, squid and cuttlefish have 8 arms which are muscular and lined with suction cups. They are used to taste their environment, manipulate objects, and hold on to prey.

Bacteria Bacteria are small organisms that live all over the world, even on and in our bodies. They are single-celled organisms that do not have the same internal complexity as animal and plant cells. Some of them help us and some of them can make us sick.

Beak Much like birds, cephalopods have beaks for mouths! The beak is located in the center of the arms and/or tentacles.

Belemnite Belemnites were the ancestors of modern day squid and cuttlefish.

Bioluminescence Many organisms create light! This light can be created by either the animals' cells or from beneficial bacteria that live in symbiosis with the animal.

Buoyancy Buoyancy is the ability to float, or in the case of cuttlefish, remain "neutrally buoyant". Being neutrally buoyant means neither floating nor sinking, just staying wherever an animal is in the water.

Cephalopod The cephalopods are actively swimming marine invertebrates within the phylum Mollusca. They include squid, octopus, nautilus, cuttlefish.

Chromatophores Many cephalopods can change the color of their skin and they are able to do that thanks in part to chromatophores! These cells have a small sack of pigment in the center of a ring of muscles that can stretch the pigment sack so that color is visible, or leave the pigment as a small ball so that the cephalopod's skin stays white.

Cirri Nautiluses have many cirri which can firmly attach to prey items. They are similar to tentacles but are not as flexible.

Cuttlebone Cuttlefish have cuttlebones which give their body structure and help them stay at a steady depth in the water. If they didn't have a cuttlebone they would have to actively swim to stay up in the water. This allows the cuttlefish to use less energy when swimming or floating above the seafloor. Cuttlebones are made of aragonite and get larger in layers as the cuttlefish grows!

Jet propulsion Many cephalopods move using a combination of fin flapping and pushing water forcefully through their siphon, which is called jet propulsion!

Mantle The mantle is the body of a cephalopod from the end of the head to the back of the fins. Most organs are located in the mantle.

Marine snow The deep sea is constantly being "snowed" upon by dead organisms, mucous, and poop from animals that live above them in the seawater. When humans observed these falling pieces of marine life, it looked like snow, and thus the term "marine snow" was born. Many animals subsist solely off marine snow, like the Vampire squid!

Papillae Some cephalopods are able to change the texture of their skin using collections of muscles called papillae. They can push the skin up into extreme structures so that the cephalopod can look more like a rough coral or rock.

Photophore Photophores are specialized organs in some squid and other animals where bioluminescence occurs.

Radula The radula is similar to our tongue! The difference, of course, is that the squid's radula is covered in tiny teeth that rip apart their prey.

Seagrass Seagrass is a flowering plant that lives underwater! This plant looks just like tall grasses you might see on land. Seagrass beds are very important habitats for many young animals because they offer a place for animals to hide from predators!

Sexual dimorphism When the males and females of the same species look different from each other, this is called sexual dimorphism.

Siphon The siphon is the muscular tube through which cephalopods force water when using jet propulsion to swim.

Symbiosis When two organisms live together, this is called symbiosis. There are 3 kinds of symbiosis. Mutualism, in which both partners benefit from the relationship, commensalism, in which one partner benefits and the other is indifferent, and parasitism, in which one partner benefits and the other is harmed.

Tentacle Cuttlefish and squid have specialized appendages that are super stretchy for catching prey. The ends of the tentacles have clubs with teeth-rimmed suckers that allow them to dig into prey.

﹤コ:彡　　Acknowledgements　　﹤コ:彡

Thank you to my fellow cephalopod biologists Dr. Danna Staaf (@DannaStaaf) and Casey Zakroff (@CaseyZakroff), for editing this book with extreme attention to detail.

Thank you to my friends who edited this book, including Dorothy "Darshu" Gibbons, David Jenkins (@dfjenkins3), Dustin Growick (twitter @DustinGrowick Instagram @DinosaurWhisperer), Zak Martellucci (twitter @ZakMartellucci instagram @zzzzzzak), Andrea Suria (@ASuria25), Nick Yarmey (@NickYarmey), Henry Frye, JD Tamucci(@jc_tamucci), Jesse Lee, Deirdre Halloran, Patrick Clarke, and Caitlin Casey.

Thank you to folks who helped me edit, including Mariah Loeber, Flavia Huber, and *especially* Anna Scharnagl (@AnnaScharnagl).

Thank you to my Ph.D. advisor, Dr. Spencer Nyholm (@SpencerNyholm), who doesn't get mad at me for spending time on science communication.

Made in the USA
Lexington, KY
02 December 2018